PIANO SOLO

DAVID LANZ
HERE COMES THE SUN

You can hear the solo piano and ensemble recording at:
DavidLanz.com/HCTS

For more information on the music and other artists featured on the *Here Comes the Sun* album,
visit **DavidLanz.com**

Cover artwork designed by Daniela Boifava
daniela@visiongate.com

Special thanks to Kathy Parsons
MainlyPiano.com

ISBN 978-1-4584-1963-7

HAL•LEONARD®
CORPORATION
7777 W. BLUEMOUND RD. P.O. BOX 13819 MILWAUKEE, WI 53213

Visit Hal Leonard Online at
www.halleonard.com

There are far too many great Beatle songs to do a proper tribute on a single recording or in a solitary songbook. This was the creative dilemma faced after the release of *Liverpool Re-Imagining the Beatles*, where the focus was placed solely on arrangements from the John Lennon and Paul McCartney songbook. However, now on *Here Comes The Sun*, the spotlight has been widened to include the other great Beatle songwriter, George Harrison.

His presence is obvious on the title track, but is also heard on *Sir George*, a musical tribute I initially began composing during the making of *Liverpool*, and then later completed to be included in this project.

Lennon and McCartney songs still make up the lion's share of the repertoire ranging from their innocent early days, *There's A Place* and *Please Please Me*, to their more mature, studio savvy period, notably *Penny Lane* and *I Am The Walrus*.

The Beatles, of course, have had a tremendous impact on musicians and composers of my generation. I cannot imagine what my own compositions and musical style would be like without their influence and without the cultural impact of the 1960's and 70's, which they were so much a part of individually and collectively. I must here once again echo my own words when I say that these songs, "have been arranged and re-imagined through the lens of my own musical voice, reflecting this great and enduring legacy of musical history".

I am also forever indebted to the other George, Sir George Martin, the brilliant producer and arranger who was arguably the "fifth Beatle" helping them greatly expand their musical reach and guiding their revolutionary use of the recording studio.

With that in mind, *Sir George*, seemed a fitting musical conclusion to this nearly four year arranging and recording odyssey, and with its apropos subtitle, *Liverpool Farewell*, we complete this chapter and tribute to an era of music that continues to live on and inspire. Here's to the world's greatest, the one and only Beatles!

David Lanz

PRELUDE: SUNRISE FOLLOWS MOON

By DAVID LANZ

Moderately slow, with freedom

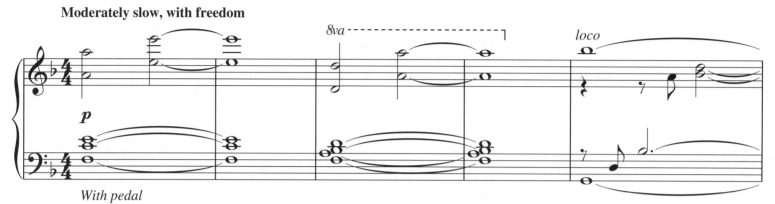

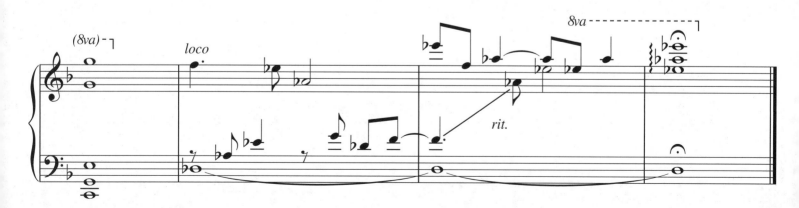

HERE COMES THE SUN

Words and Music by
GEORGE HARRISON

Moderately

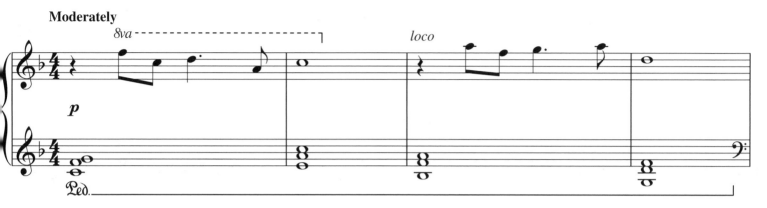

Pedal as needed

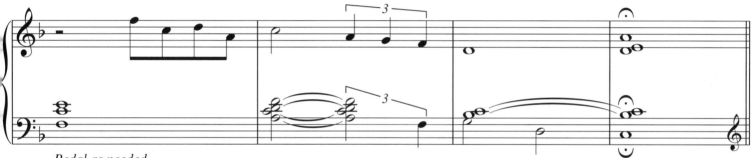

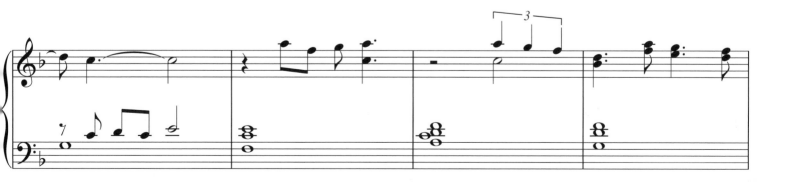

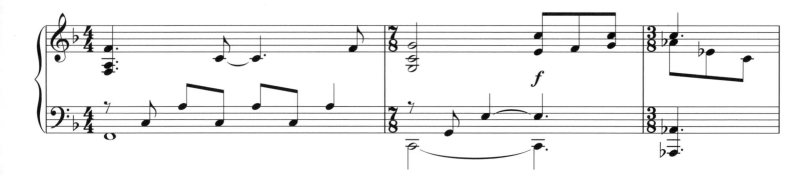

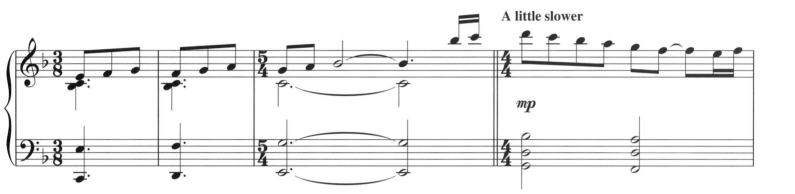

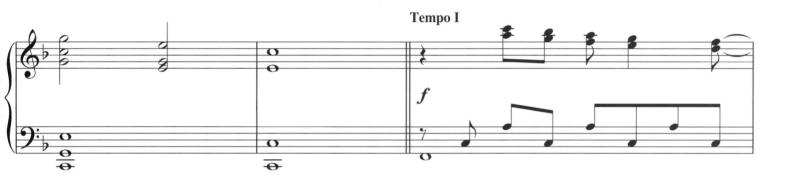

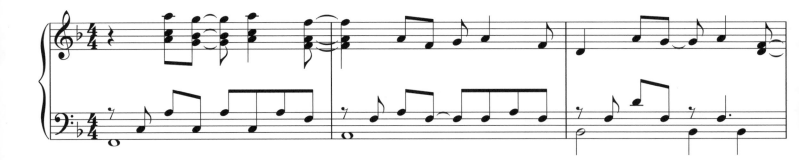

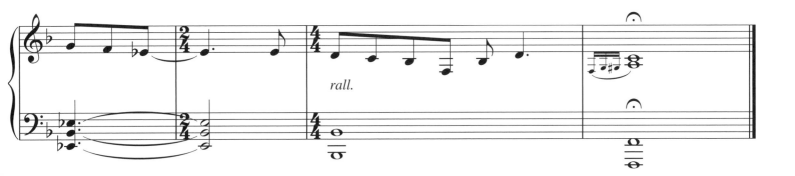

HELP!

Words and Music by JOHN LENNON
and PAUL McCARTNEY

Freely

Moderately

bring out L.H. melody

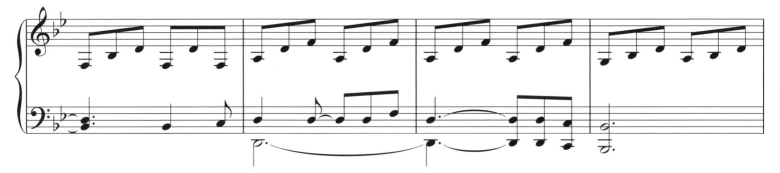

8vb

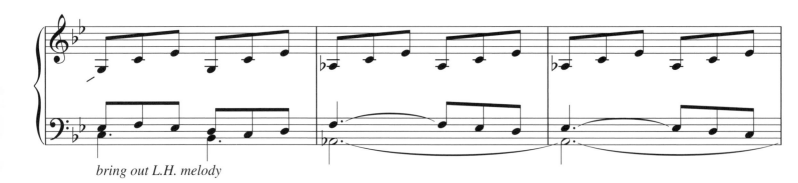

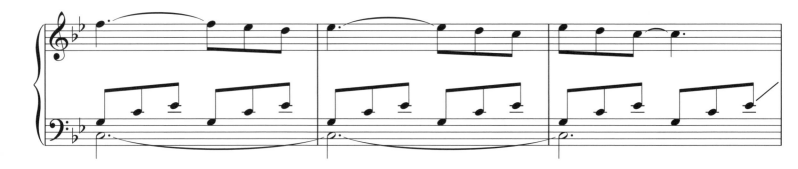

bring out L.H. melody

bring out
L.H. melody

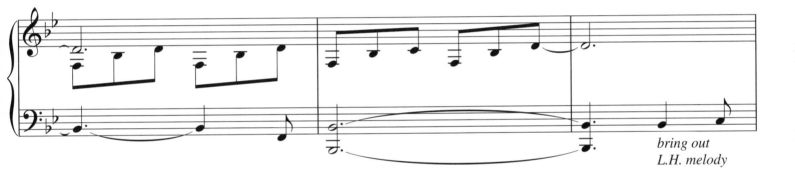

8vb

bring out L.H. melody

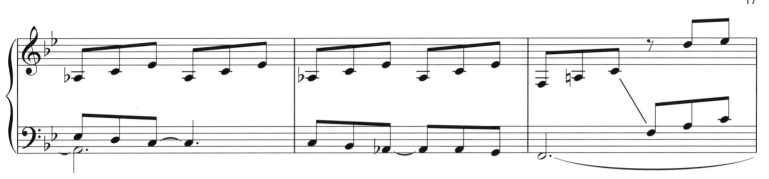

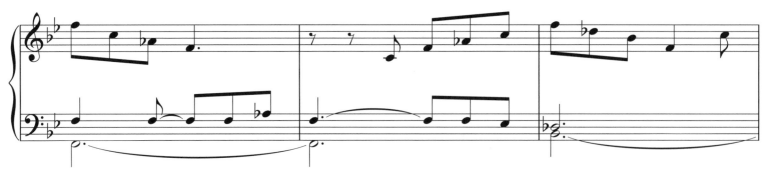

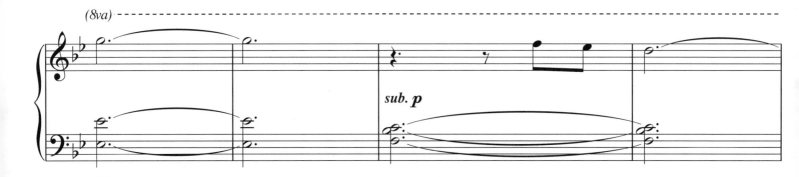

bring out L.H. melody

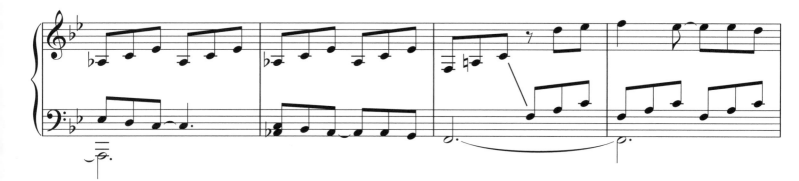

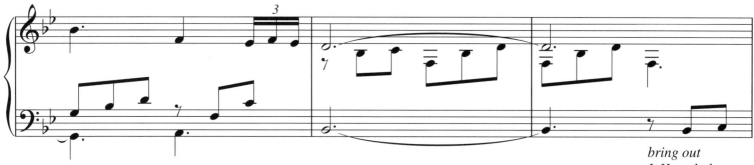

bring out
L.H. melody

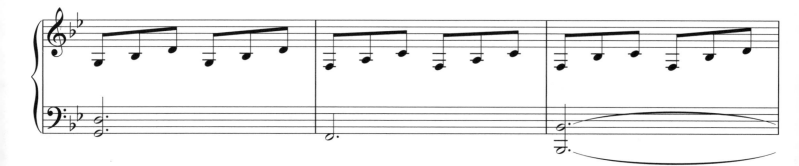

MOTHER NATURE'S SON

Words and Music by JOHN LENNON
and PAUL McCARTNEY

Moderately, with freedom

With pedal

bring out L.H. melody

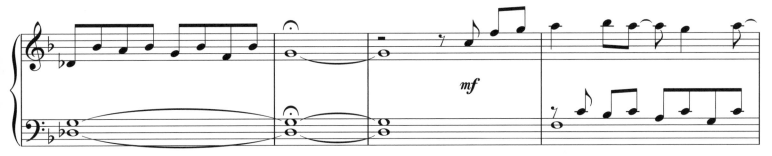

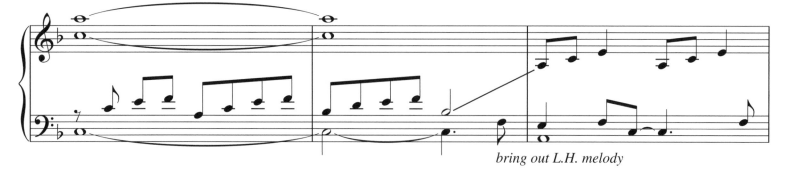

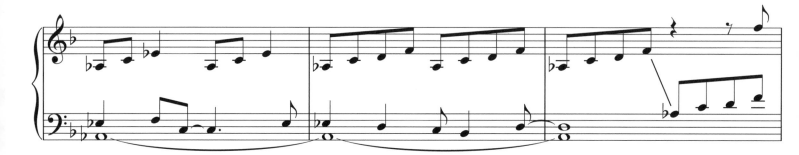

bring out L.H. melody

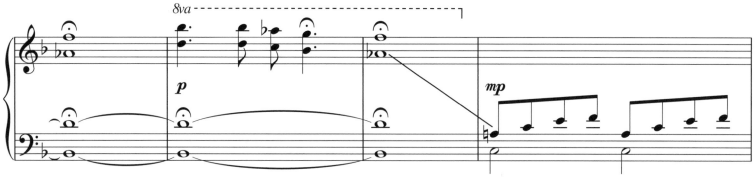

bring out L.H. melody

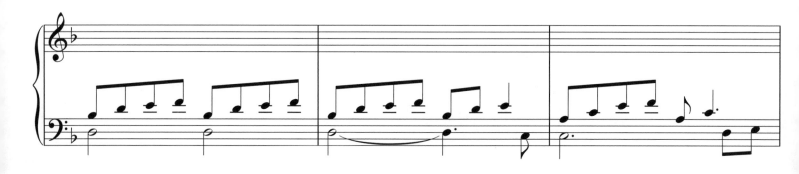

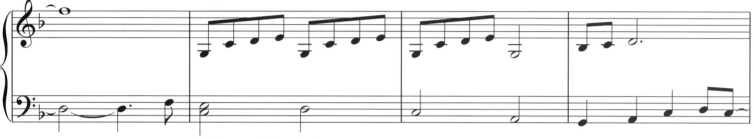

bring out L.H. melody

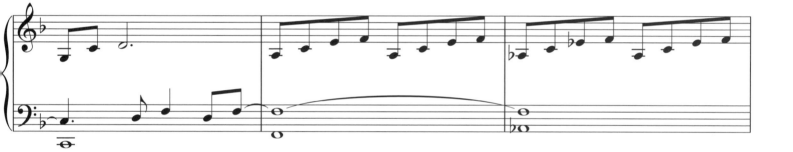

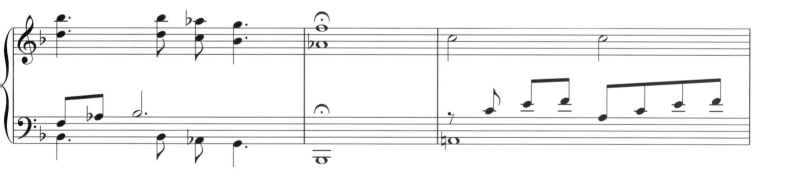

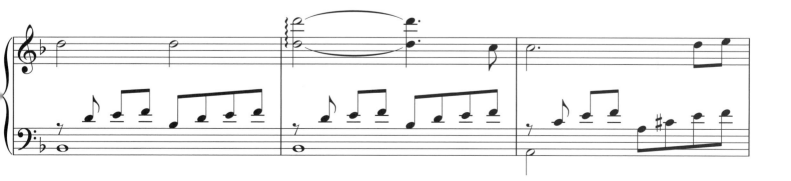

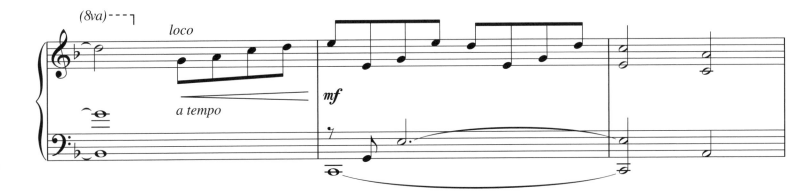

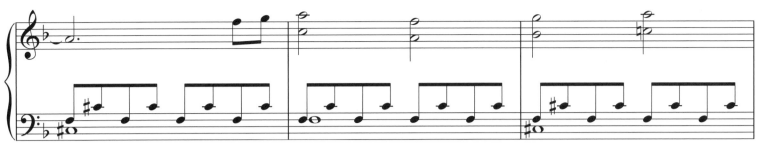

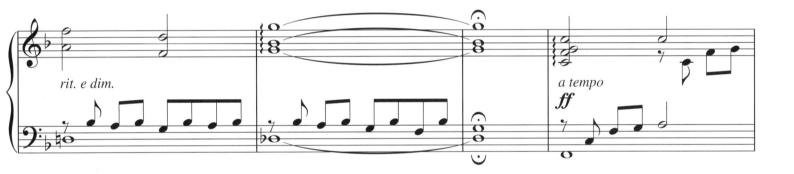

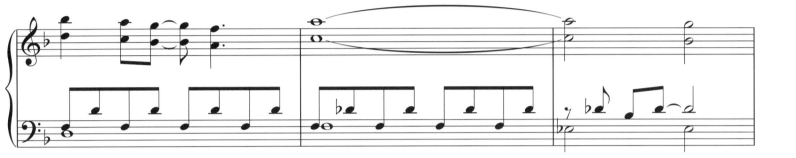

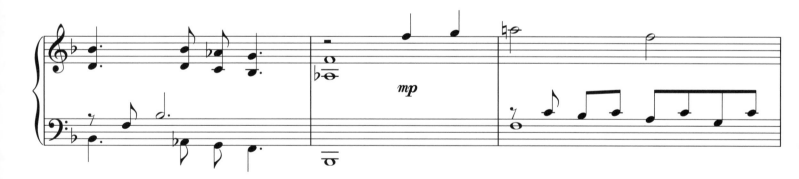

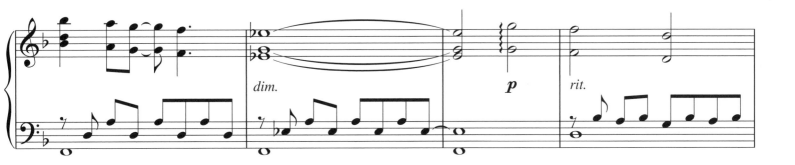

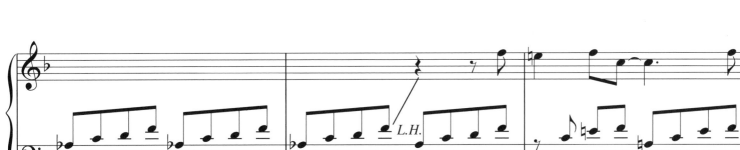

bring out L.H. melody

bring out
L.H. melody

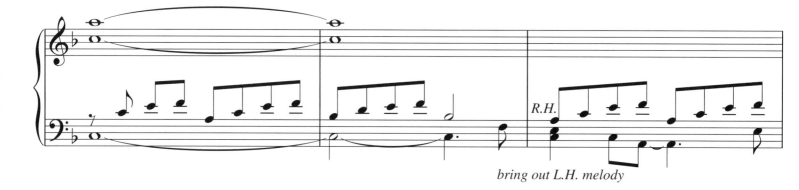

bring out L.H. melody

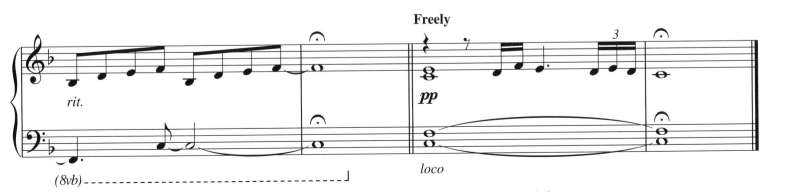

FOR NO ONE

Words and Music by JOHN LENNON
and PAUL McCARTNEY

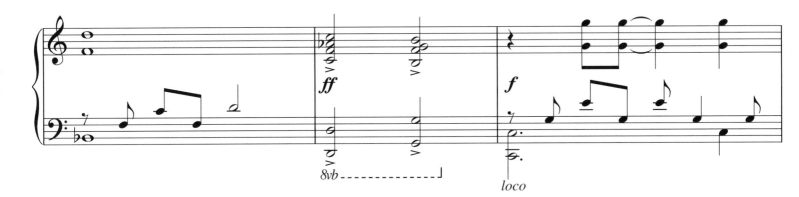

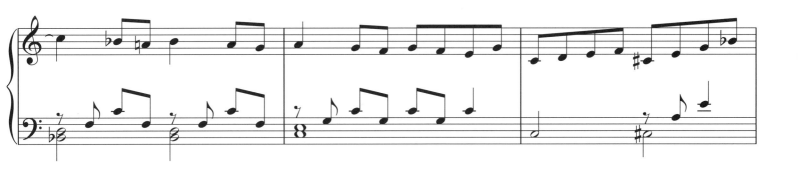

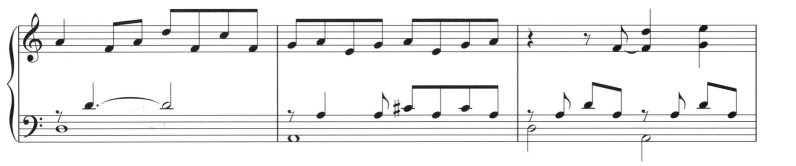

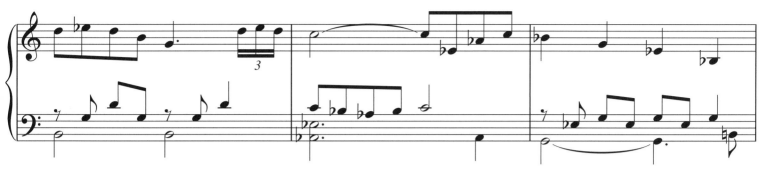

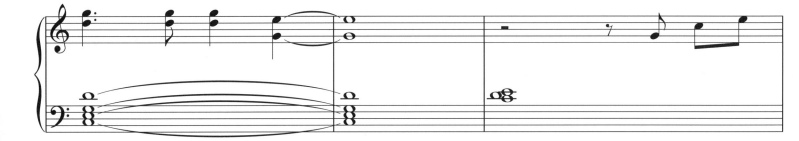

THERE'S A PLACE

Words and Music by JOHN LENNON
and PAUL McCARTNEY

Moderately

Opt.: R.H. over

With pedal

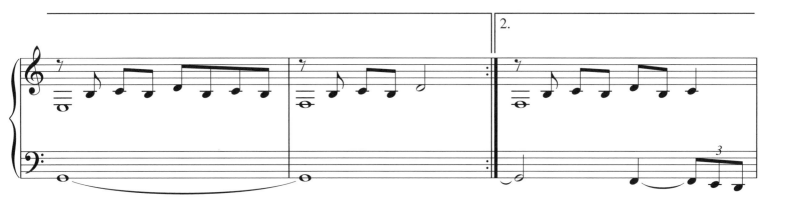

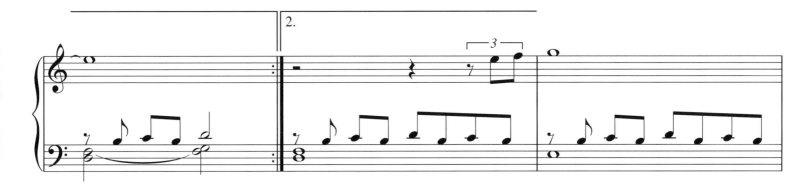

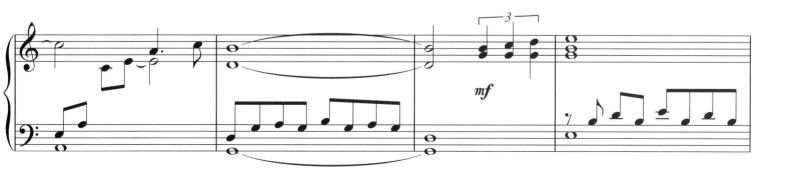

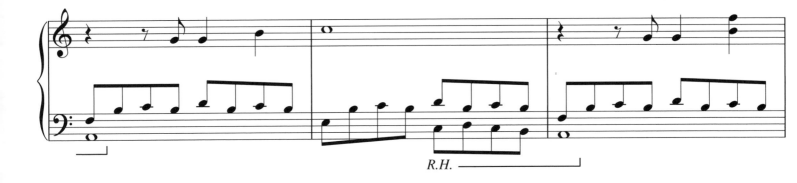

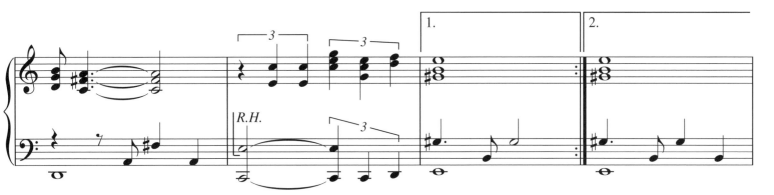

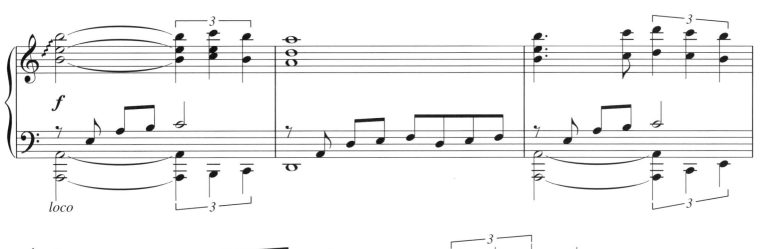

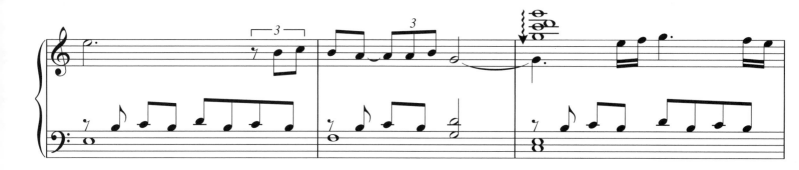

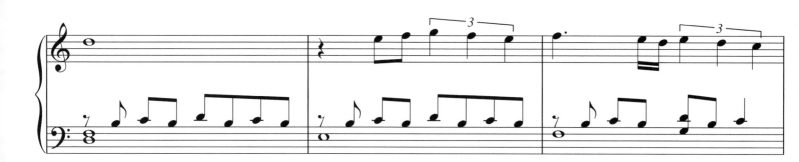

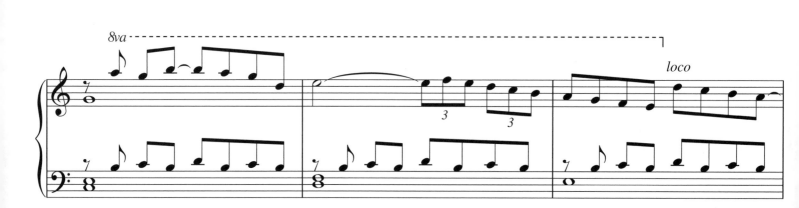

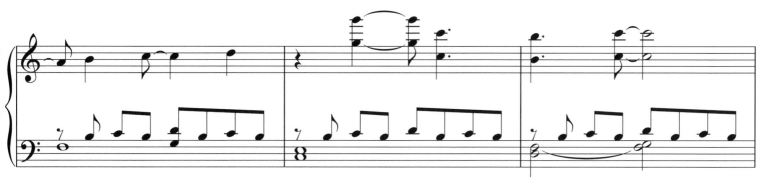

bring out L.H. melody

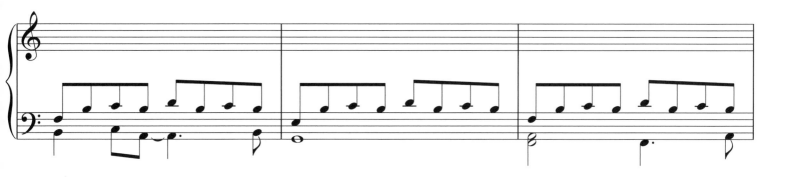

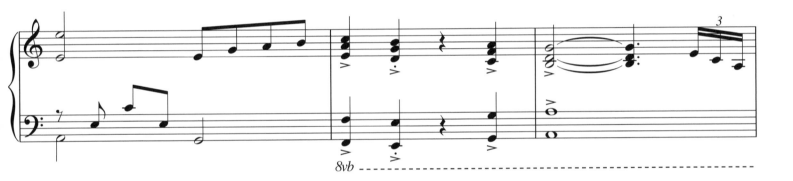

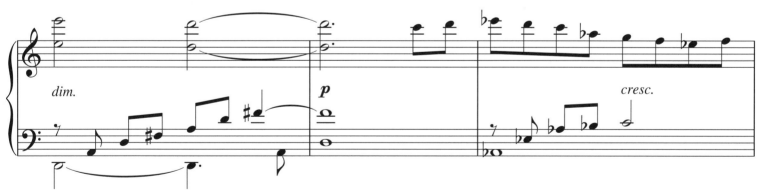

PLEASE PLEASE ME

Words and Music by JOHN LENNON
and PAUL McCARTNEY

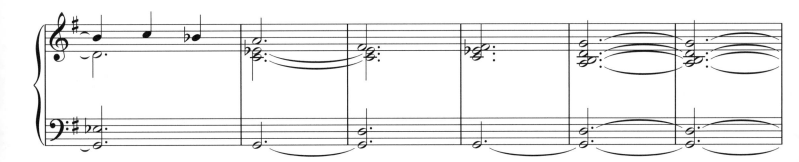

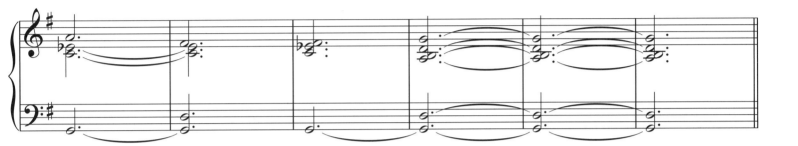

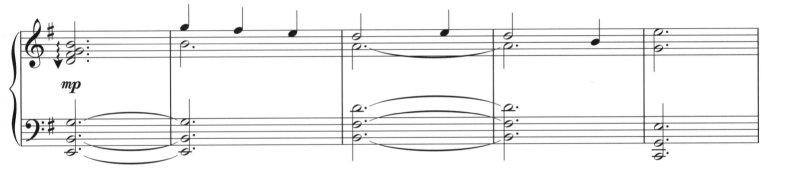

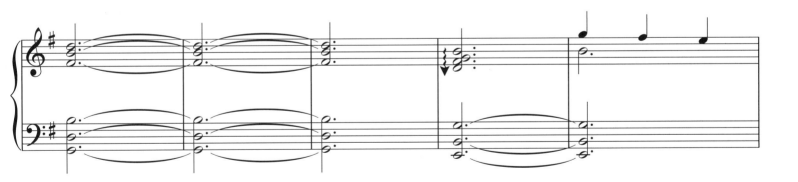

* Pianists with smaller hands can roll the chords from
bottom to top, remove the top notes of the chords, or play octaves.

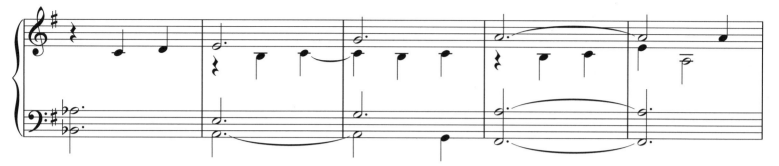

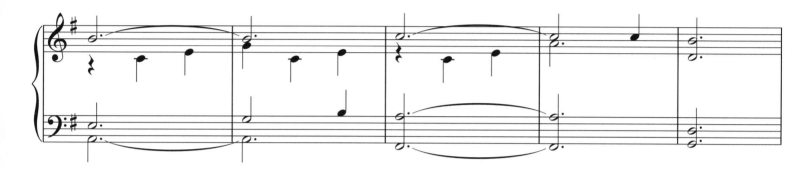

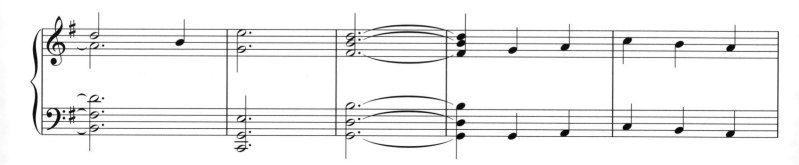

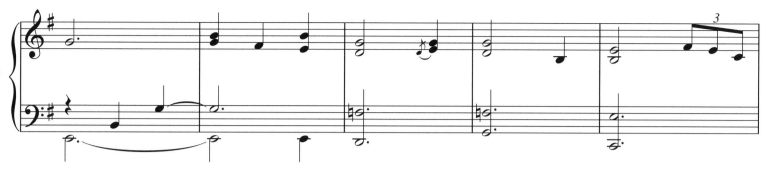

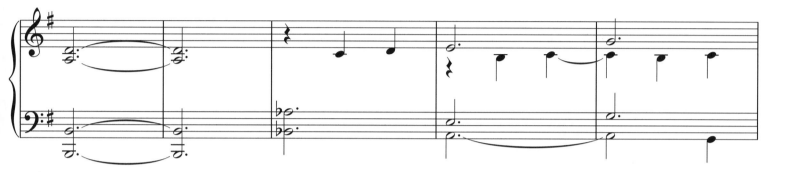

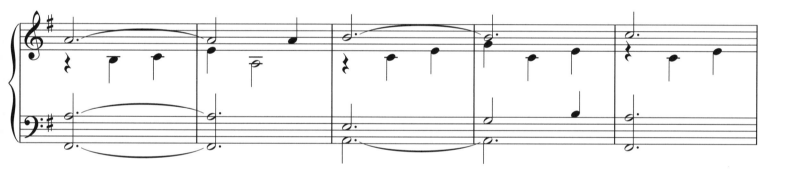

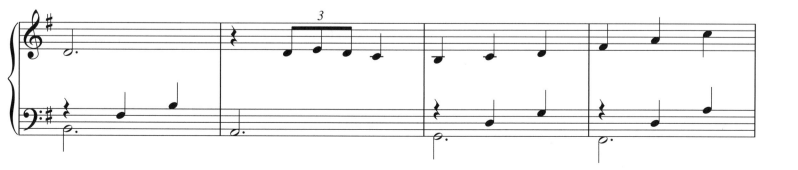

54

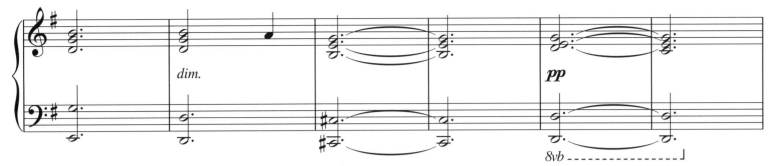

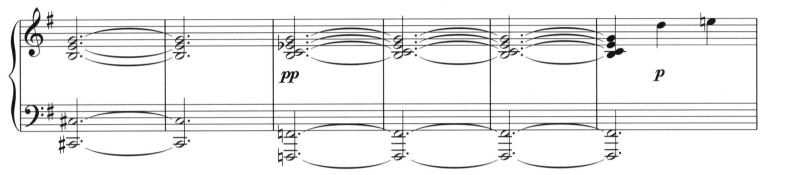

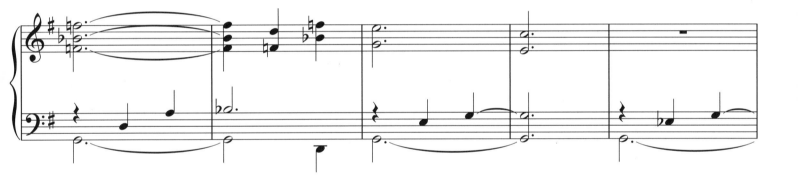

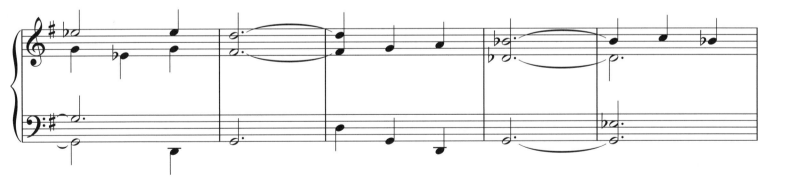

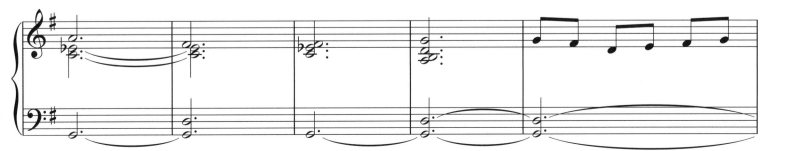

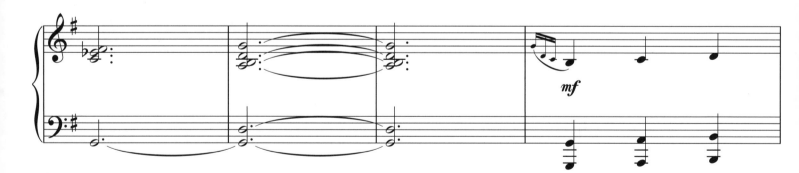

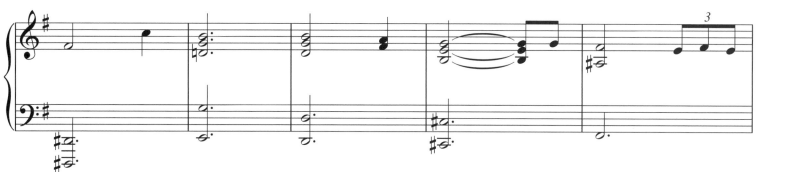

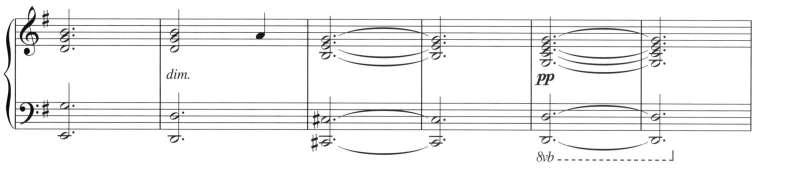

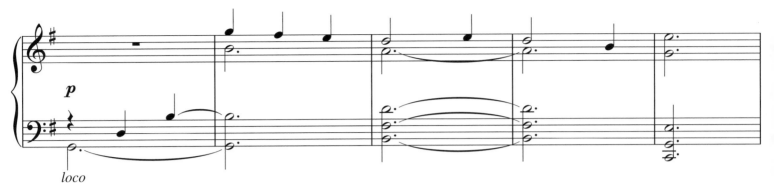

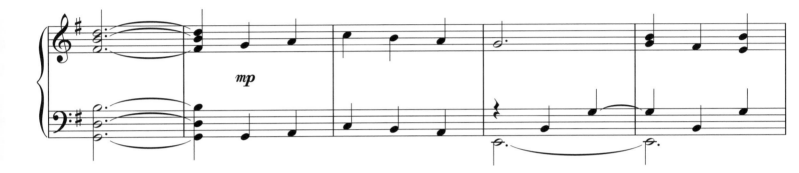

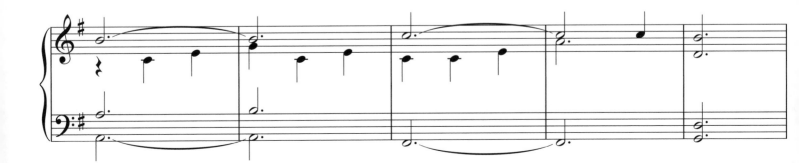

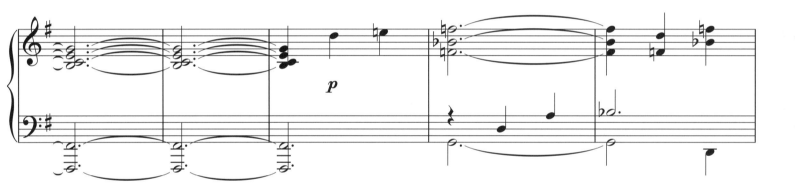

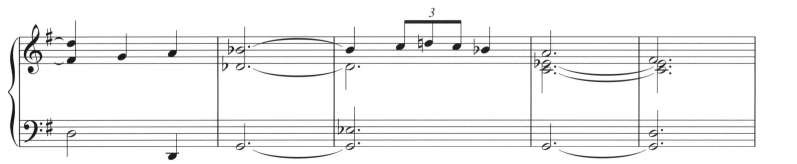

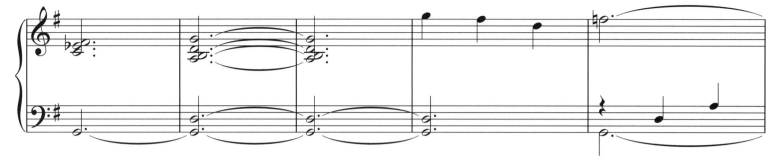

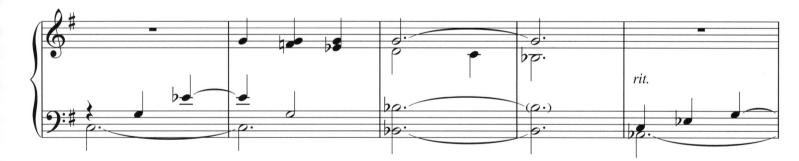

rit.

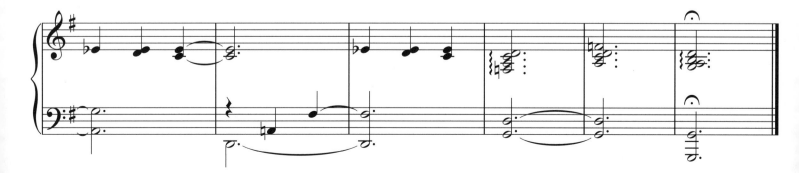

PENNY LANE

Words and Music by JOHN LENNON
and PAUL McCARTNEY

Slowly and Freely

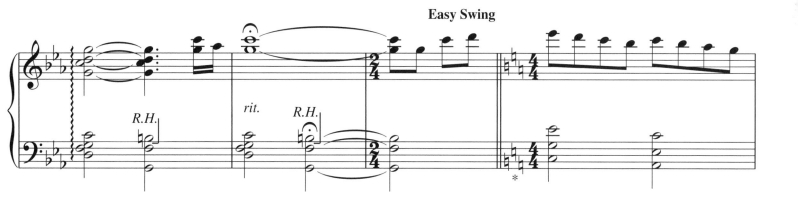

* *Pianists with smaller hands can play
octaves from bottom notes of L.H. chords.*

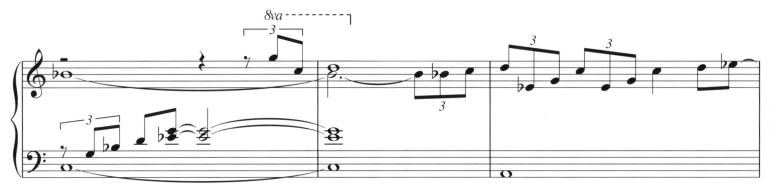

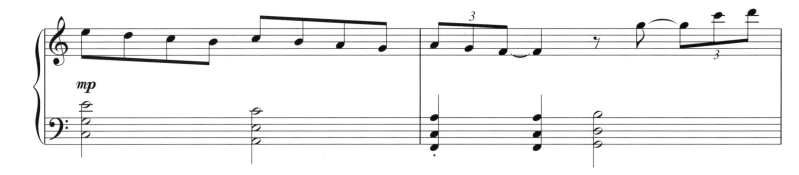

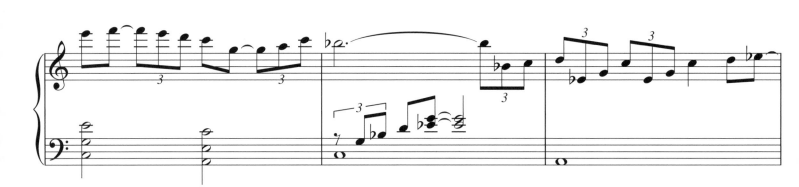

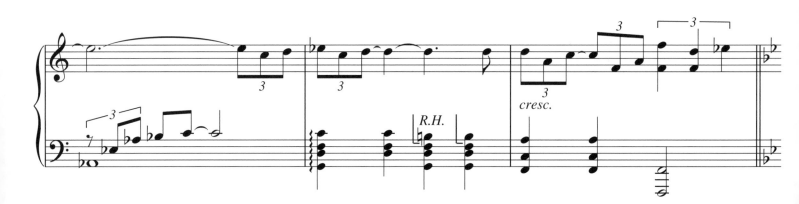

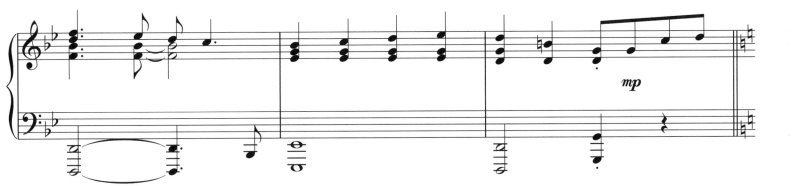

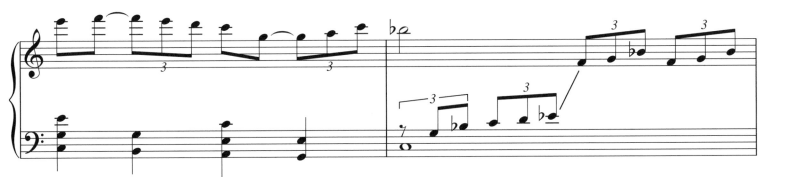

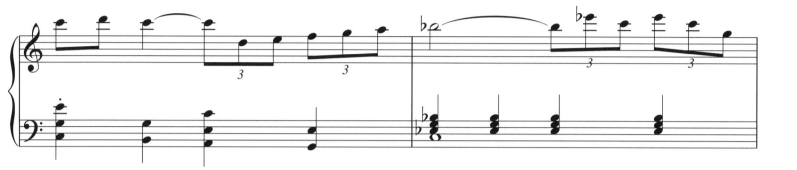

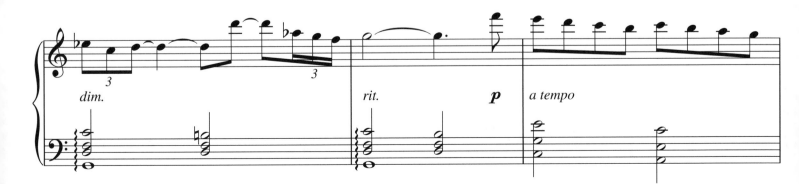

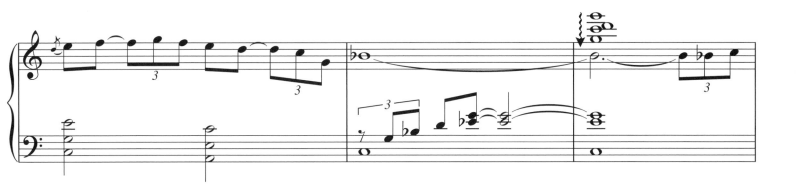

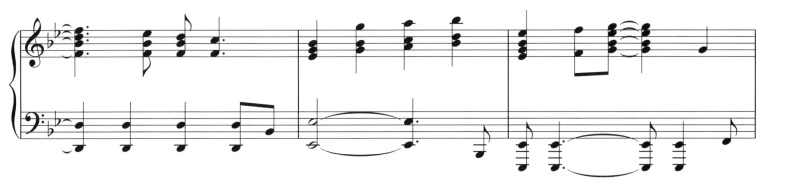

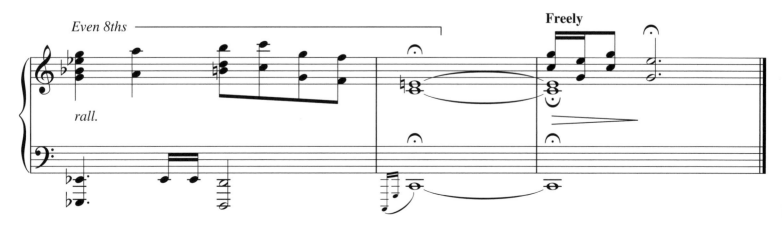

I AM THE WALRUS

Words and Music by JOHN LENNON
and PAUL McCARTNEY

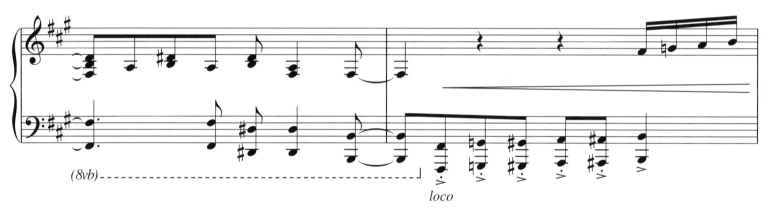

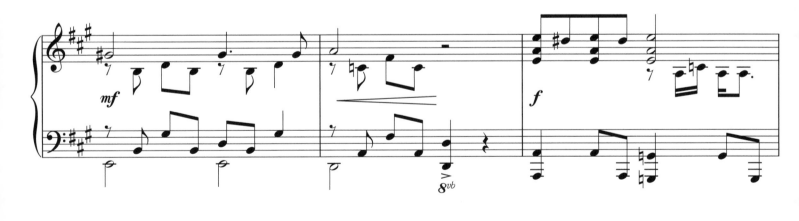

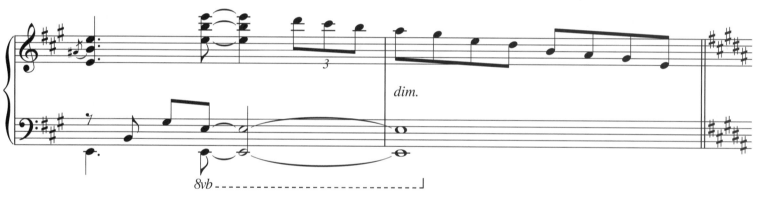

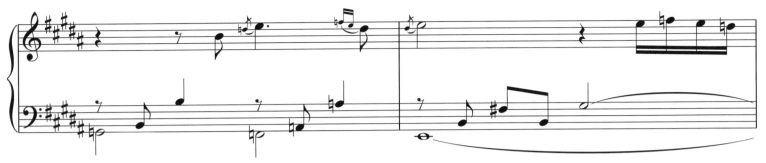

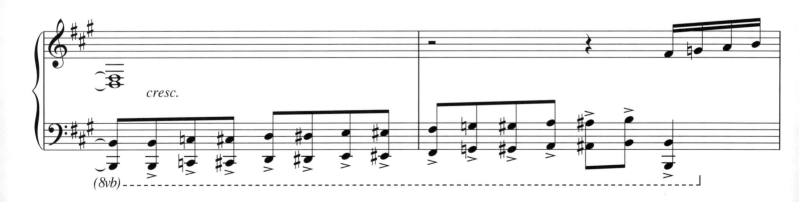

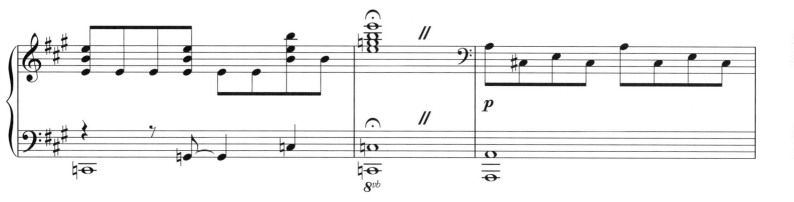

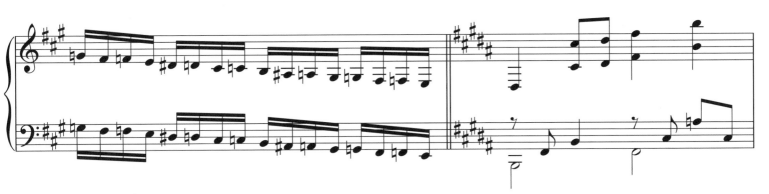

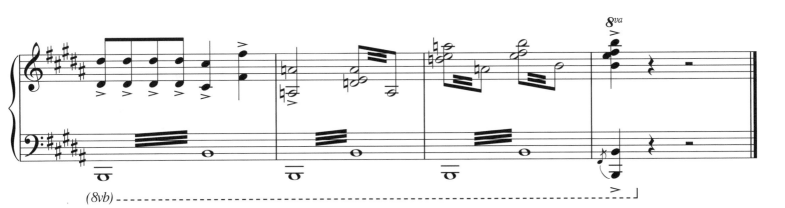

SIR GEORGE

By DAVID LANZ

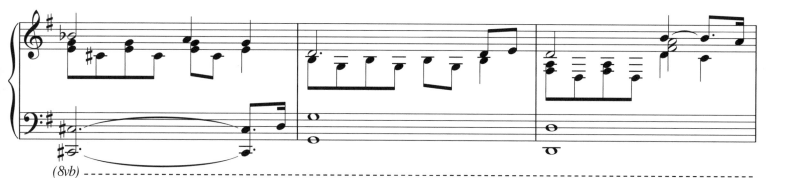

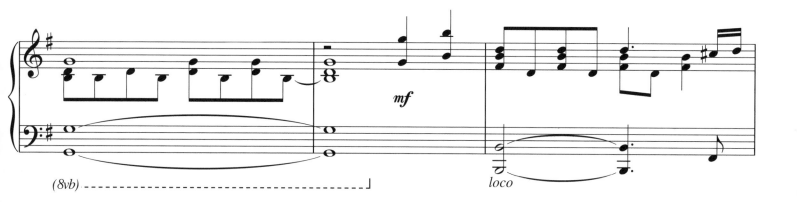

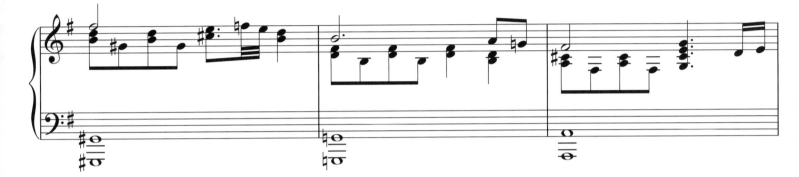

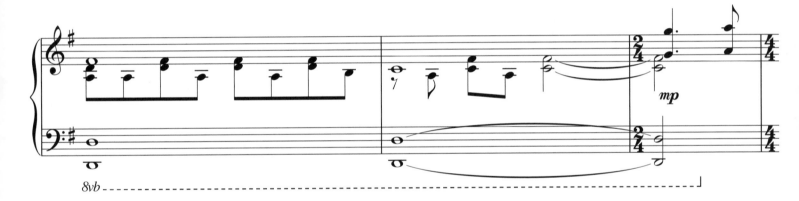

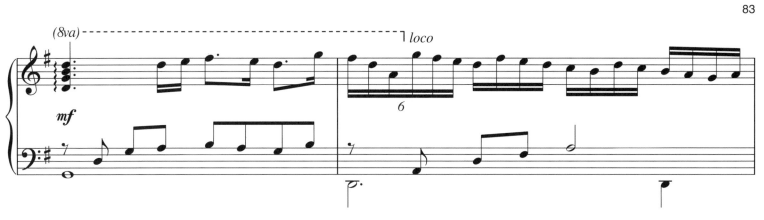

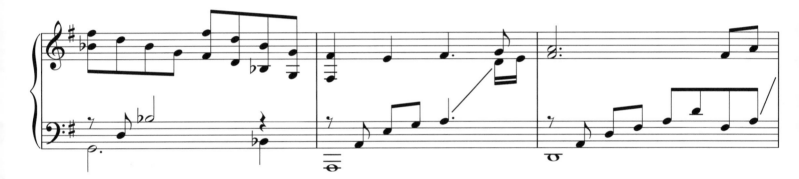

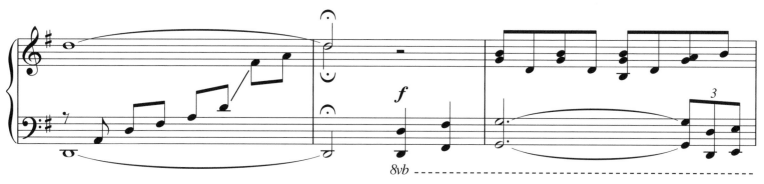

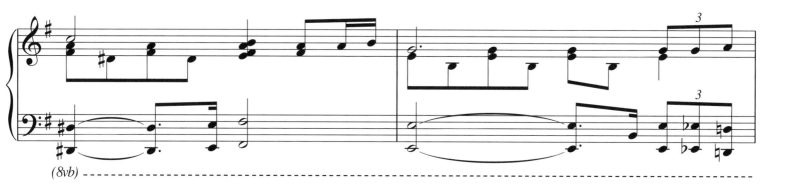

Also available from David Lanz and Hal Leonard Corporation:

LIVERPOOL · RE-IMAGINING THE BEATLES